OPERA CITY

COURT CASTLE

IC4 DESIGN

CATCH UP WITH MISTER X

DRINK COOL COLA · 5¢ · 5¢

1922

Traveling Circus
Emma & Tomo & Seisho
SUNDAY MUSICAL

DANCE CHALLENGE
YOU'RE INVITED!

THUNDERSTRUCK

MAZE THEATRE — SIGN STREET

PIGGY PIZZA

TACO-SHELL
MOTOR OIL

The Opera City Times

Pirates of The Rock Castle Fortress

1900

STAR COFFEE CO.

LIVE IT UP! MISTER

"The Phantom Thief"

X

THE DETECTIVE BUREAU

PIERRE & CARMEN

BIG SUNNY MOUNTAIN RAILROAD CO., LTD

Pierre The MAZE DETECTIVE

The Search for the Stolen Maze Stone

By

HIRO KAMIGAKI
&
IC4DESIGN

Written by CHIHIRO MARUYAMA
Translation by EMMA SAKAMIYA
& ELIZABETH JENNER

Laurence King Publishing

HOW TO PLAY

1 First, find the **START** ················> START
Follow the maze until you find *Mr X*
who will be next to the **GOAL** ·········> GOAL

2 On each maze, solve **EXTRA CHALLENGES** from *Mr X* and respond to written requests from other characters.

3 Try to **FIND** gold stars, red trophies, green and red treasure chests and other **HIDDEN OBJECTS** in each of the mazes.

4 If the course is **BLOCKED**, find an alternative route. You can walk past a person or animal on a path only if there is room to pass them. If there is more than one possible course, choose the **SHORTEST**.  ✓ ✗

PICTURE THE SCENE...

There is a street on the outskirts of Opera City.

On this street stands a sturdy red-brick garage nestled low-down in the urban valley of buildings. It is a slightly odd place to call home. Yet this is where Pierre, the Maze Detective, lives. Inside Pierre nonchalantly sips his tea and hums a tune, waiting for a new case to turn up. Even when an incident occurs, Pierre is rarely called upon as he is a specialist ... the solver of mazes **... A MAZE DETECTIVE!**

Pierre
The Maze
Detective

Carmen
Pierre's friend

Mr X
The Phantom
Thief

Pierre's Garage

Pierre's friend Carmen bursts into the garage in great excitement. A major crime has occurred! In her hand, Carmen is gripping a letter from Mr X and a newspaper that outlines the incident. There is nothing else for it: only Pierre can solve this case. Why? Because he is the Maze Detective!

Mysterious Letter from Mr X

Well, my little detective friend, let battle commence!

I have hidden my first Challenge Card in your room.

Once you have the card, the chase will begin...

From X

Hidden Items

☆ 1 GOLD STAR

🏆 1 RED TROPHY

🎁 1 GREEN TREASURE CHEST

Pierre's Treasures

A model airship

A white cuddly bear

A red truck

A sun mask

The Opera City Times Vol.1

Maze Stone stolen by master criminal: Mr X the Phantom Thief!

The missing Maze Stone has the power to turn everything into a maze.

Usually that power is sealed within the Stone and the peace of the city is maintained. This theft spells serious trouble for the people of Opera City.

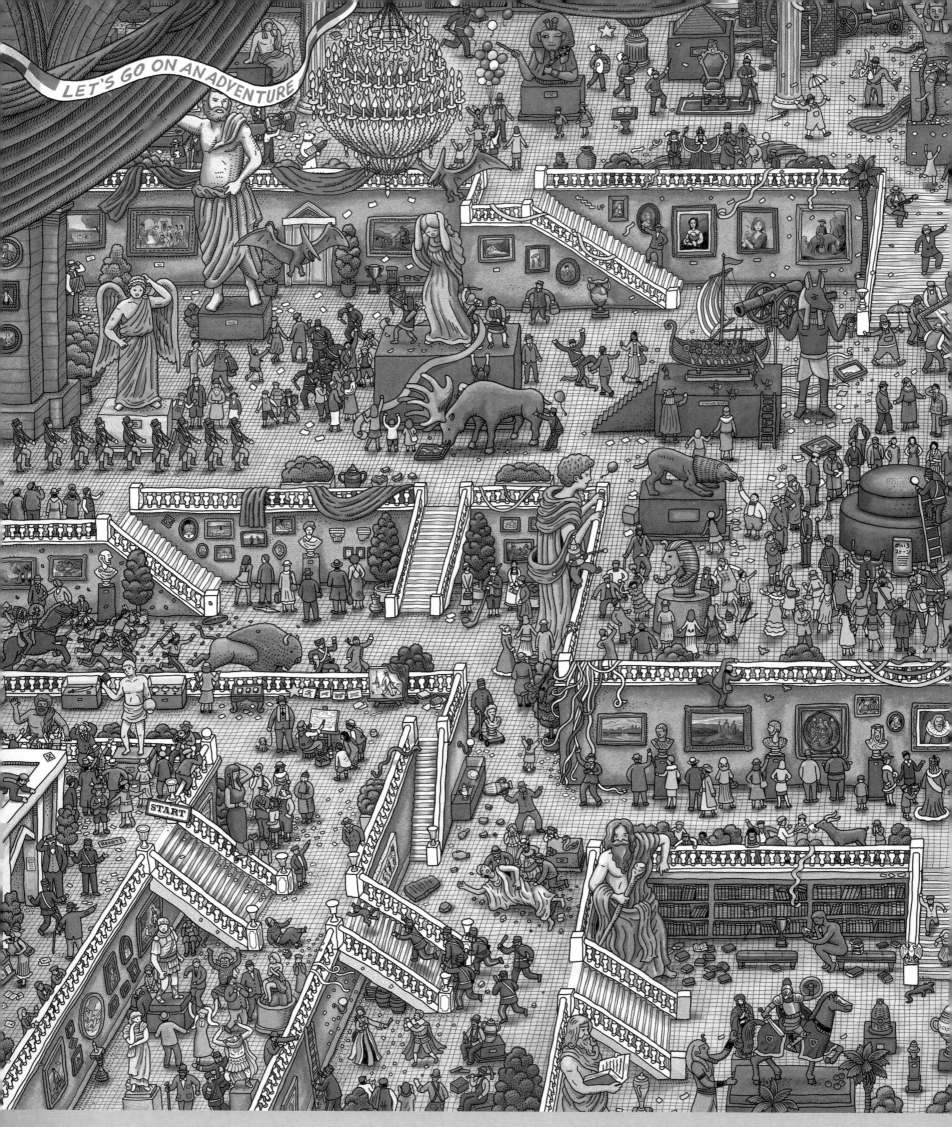

The Museum

Uh-oh! The Maze Stone has been stolen from its plinth in the middle of the museum. What a catastrophe! This will be a tricky one to solve. Move quickly down three staircases but watch out for the charging reindeer! Lend a hand with mammoth hunting and the goal will be in sight. Look! It is Mr X! He's trying to escape from the roof of the museum. Quick, follow him!

Mr X's Museum Challenge

Ha ha! I broke into the monkey cage.

Now they are on the loose – and very difficult to catch. They are masters of mischief! Once you have found the five naughty monkeys, you can advance to the next stage.

From X

Hidden Items

- ★ 5 GOLD STARS
- 🏆 3 RED TROPHIES
- 🎁 1 GREEN TREASURE CHEST

MUSEUM RECOMMENDS

GREEN DINOSAUR
SAMURAI ARMOUR
CAST-IRON CANNON
A VIKING SHIP
A KING'S RED THRONE

UNMISSABLE!

Museum Director's REQUEST

Where has the scatterbrained Deputy Director gone?

He's wearing a red suit and a sky blue shirt.

The Town
Makes Merry

Disaster! Mr X has escaped into the town, where things look very lively indeed. Today is a special day of celebration; it is carnival day! The Maze Detective's work starts with jumping down from the museum roof. But where is Mr X? Try passing around the four big buildings to reach the goal.

Mr X's Town Challenge

Look out for the suspicious cars that my sidekicks are driving. Find five cars marked X in order to advance to the next stage.

From X

Hidden Items

☆ 4 GOLD STARS

🏆 3 RED TROPHIES

▣ 2 GREEN TREASURE CHESTS

OPERA CITY TOURIST ATTRACTIONS

Be sure not to miss:

- the fountain
- a red sightseeing bus
- the pole-climbing competition
- the rooftop café
- Bear Square
- the observation tower with circular windows

POLICE INSPECTOR'S APPEAL

There has been a bank robbery! Where on earth is the robber?

Eyewitnesses say he is carrying a gun.

Open-air Café

Head up the stairs to an open-air café. What a fabulous, fun-filled place! There's a white bear relaxing at a table. Perhaps he is waiting to share a white cake with someone? Oh! It's Mr X the Phantom Thief. He's holding the Maze Stone as he goes up the steps. Quick, after him!

ITS DE MER · RESTAURANT

RICHMAN'S CAKES

SALON D

ASTROLOG
DIVINATION

GOAL

Pierre
MAZE
DETECTIVE

Café La Place
Reminder to Café Visitors

1. Do not stand on the tables.

2. Do not take the dog's food.

3. Do not sleep on the floor.

4. No ball games.

A PUZZLE

Mr Detective, I've got
a stomach ache. It hurts!
Please get me some medicine
from Santa Claus. I'm waiting
next to the men who are
playing chess.

The Opera City Times   Vol.2

Expert pickpocket Swift spotted in the Café Square!

Swift snatches precious possessions,
moving his hands as fast as a ninja.
Can you find Swift's latest victim:
a fine-looking gentleman with a bow tie?

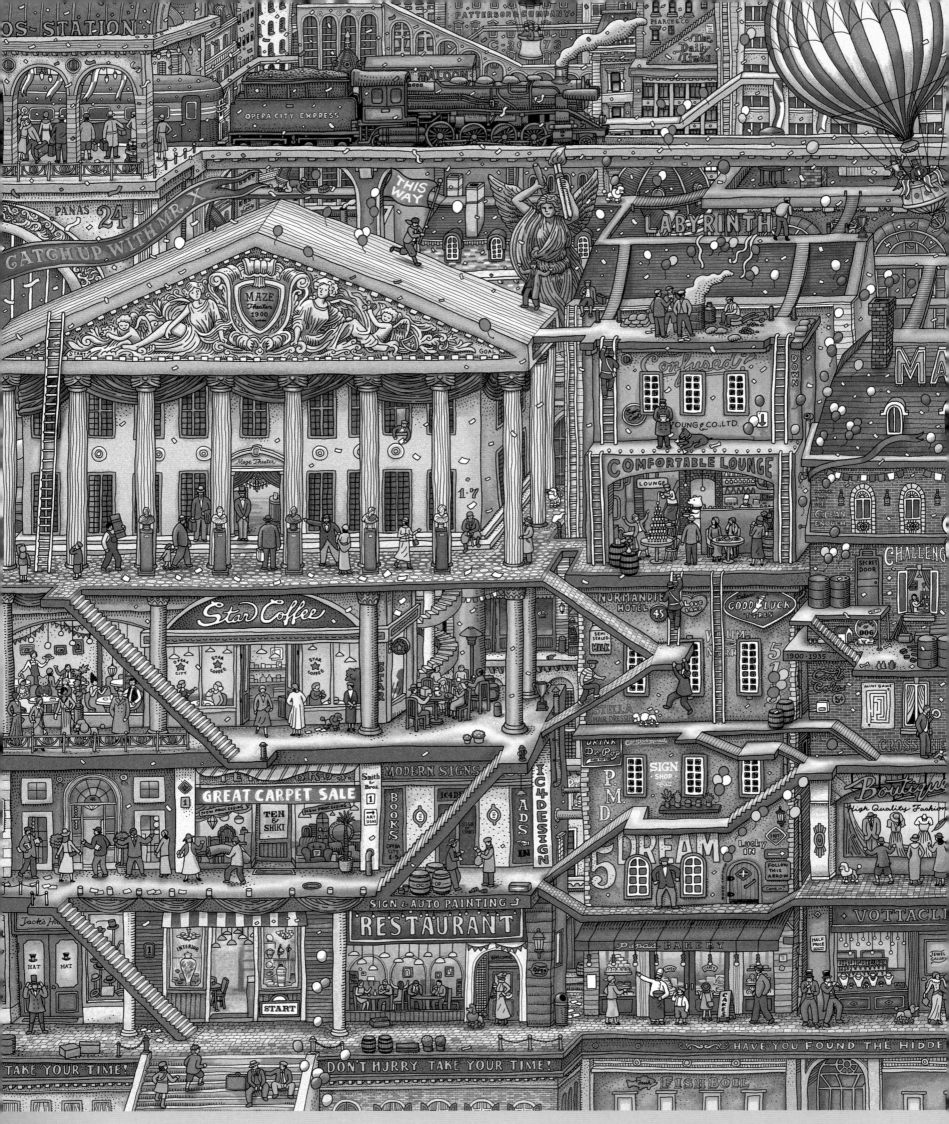

Downtown

Where are we now? In the immense wall of shops downtown – there are so many of them! Climb over the roof of the building with the pillars, then leap and bound past clothes boutiques and a flower shop until you reach the goal.

But why is there a hot-air balloon tethered to the roof? Is someone getting ready to fly away?

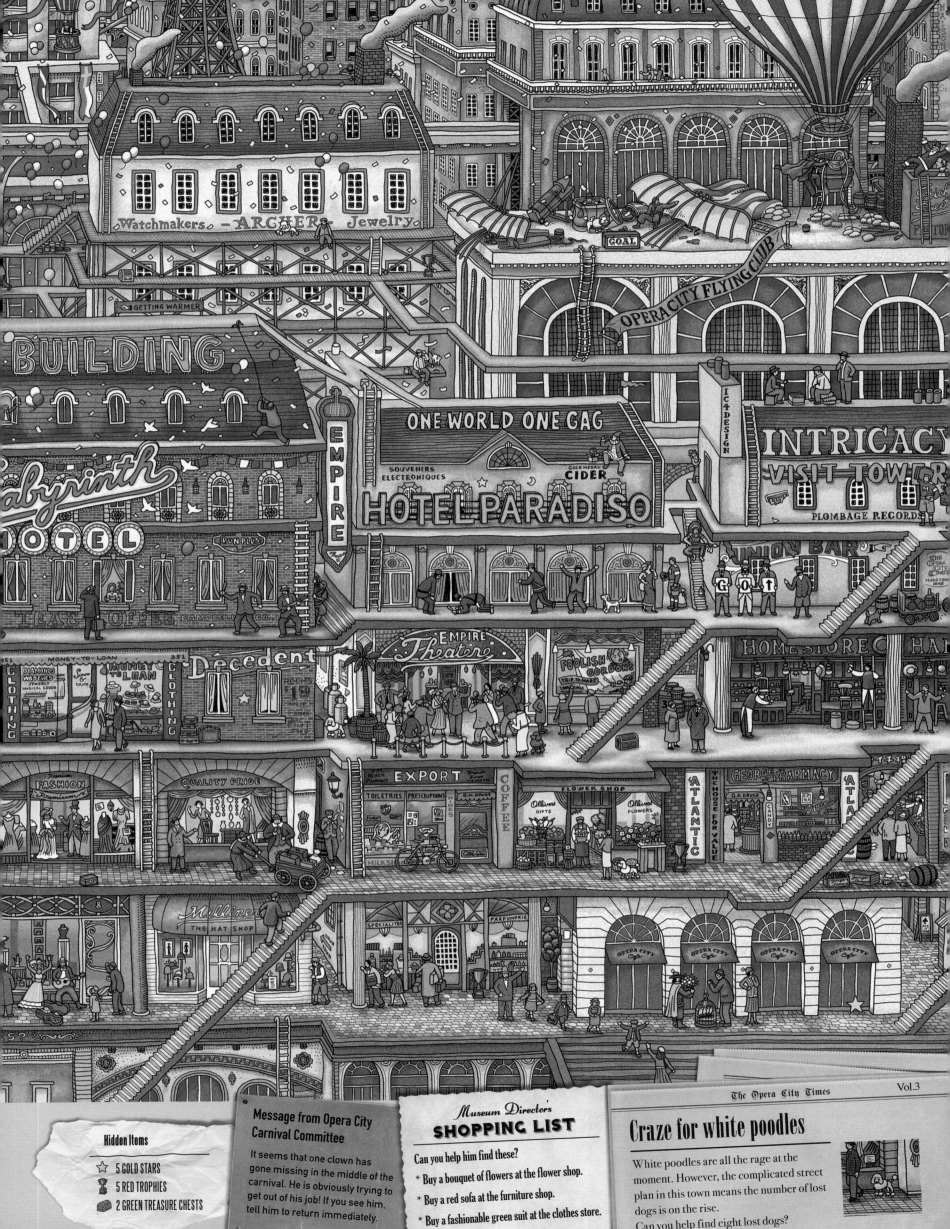

Message from Opera City Carnival Committee

It seems that one clown has gone missing in the middle of the carnival. He is obviously trying to get out of his job! If you see him, tell him to return immediately.

Museum Director's
SHOPPING LIST

Can you help him find these?

★ Buy a bouquet of flowers at the flower shop.

★ Buy a red sofa at the furniture shop.

★ Buy a fashionable green suit at the clothes store.

The Opera City Times   Vol.3

Craze for white poodles

White poodles are all the rage at the moment. However, the complicated street plan in this town means the number of lost dogs is on the rise.
Can you help find eight lost dogs?

Balloon Festival

Up, up, up and away! That explains the balloon on the shop rooftops. Now we're soaring high! Pass two gentlemen explorers flying towards the desert in search of strange creatures. Mr X can be seen floating away in the biggest balloon. Blown by the strong wind, he is making rapid progress. Where will he come down?

GOAL

Be Careful To Not Crash!

EMMA&TOMO
MUST EAT.

BALLOON ENTHUSIAST'S COMMENTS

This year's Balloon Festival is spectacular! There's a studded balloon, an ice cream-shaped balloon, and a pirate balloon with skull and crossbones. Wow! There's even a flying house! Have fun finding them!

From the Balloon Association

Today is the annual Balloon Festival. However, this year, it seems that nine aeroplanes are trying to take part. Can you find them and avert the potential danger to the festival? Thank you.

Request from a Countess

My best feather hat has been blown away in the wind.
Surely Mr X has played a trick on me.
As it is my favourite hat, please do your best to find it for me.

The Castle in the South

Wow! Take a look at this magnificent castle. What a place to land! Slide off the platform using the rope, and wind left and right down the Castle Road. Enjoy the trip across the stone bridge – it's like sailing over a sea of green. Go down the snaking path to the mouth of the forest. Mr X seems to have escaped in that direction.

Mr X's Castle Challenge

I have cast a spell over the stone soldier statues that can be found around the castle. Now, they threaten to destroy the whole town!

Find seven stone statues before advancing to the next stage.

From X

Hidden Items

☆ 6 GOLD STARS

🏆 4 RED TROPHIES

🧰 4 GREEN TREASURE CHESTS

🧰 6 RED TREASURE CHESTS

RECOMMENDATIONS FROM CASTLE TOURIST BOARD

This castle offers many great sights:

• Take a commemorative photo with the valley as a backdrop.
• Make a wish at the lion fountain.
• Spot three huge eagles flying overhead.

Peter the Goatherd says

Oh, what am I going to do?
My goats have managed to escape!
Can you help me find them?
There are ten goats in all.

The Mysterious Village in the Forest

Oh no! Poor Carmen is lost in the forest village. There's no time to hesitate. Start by climbing up to the top of the trees where the Forest Wizard lives – but don't look down! The Wizard says that Carmen has gone into a strange house deep in the forest with Mr X. Find the way down from the treetops to the stairs that lead to the house.

Hidden Items

⭐ 5 GOLD STARS

🏆 4 RED TROPHIES

📦 4 GREEN TREASURE CHESTS

📦 2 RED TREASURE CHESTS

Find out more about life in the forest

Can you spot two apprentices learning magic, and a pet gorilla? There's a forest wrestling match and a tree-climbing challenge going on. The long slide looks like lots of fun, too!

Alphabet Maze

Why don't you try the Alphabet Maze? Enter Door A at the bottom of the tree, and exit from another Door A. But make sure it leads to Door B. You must always exit from the door that leads to the next letter in the alphabet. When you reach Door E, a treasure chest awaits you!

🔑 Advice from the Forest Wizard

There are nine keys hidden in this forest. You need to collect all of them to be able to enter the strange mansion. Use your powers of concentration to find the keys.

from the Forest Wizard

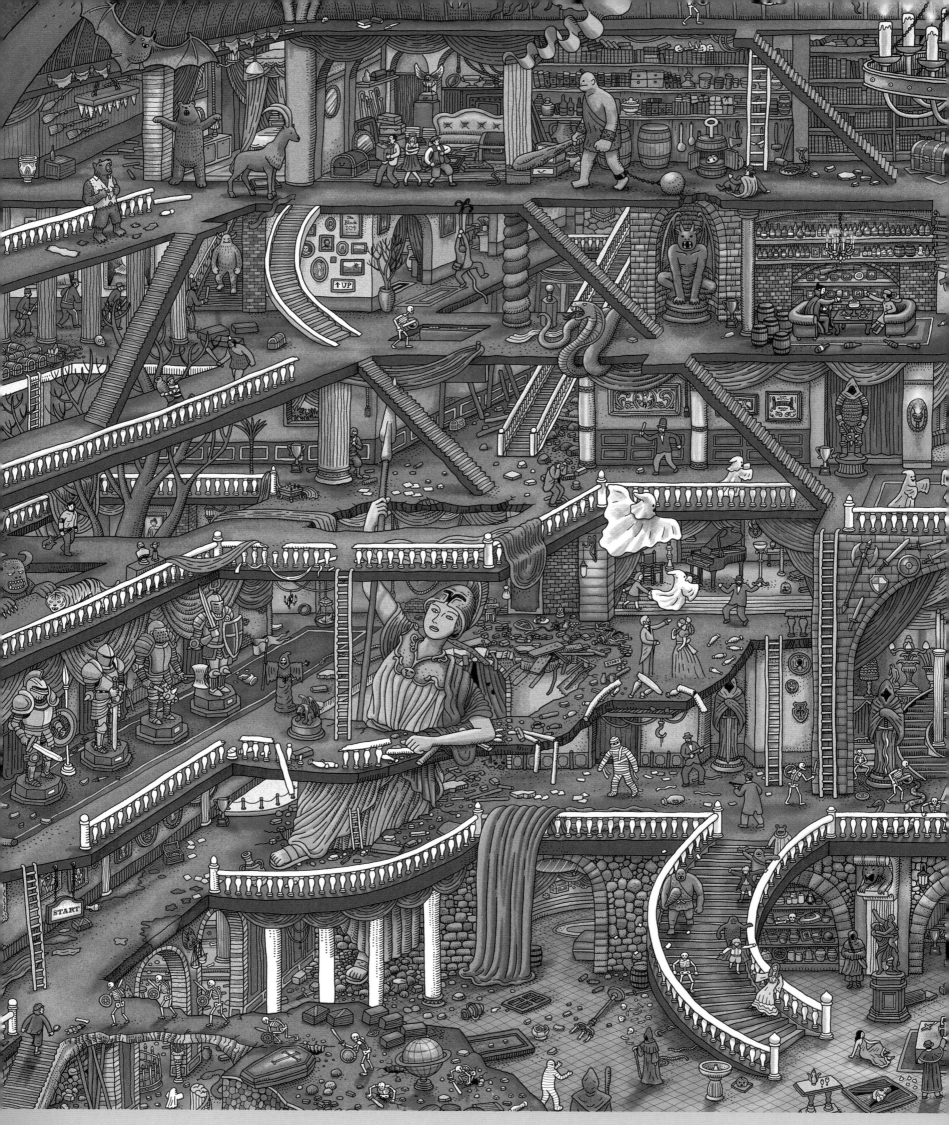

The Haunted Mansion

This is Dracula's house! It's as scary as you might imagine. Just take a look around: mummies, an army of ghosts, and skeleton knights. And – oh! It's Carmen. Unbelievably, she looks like she's having fun as she talks to Dracula. Try to grab her, then sneak through the strange ballroom and hurry to the goal. This place is creepy!

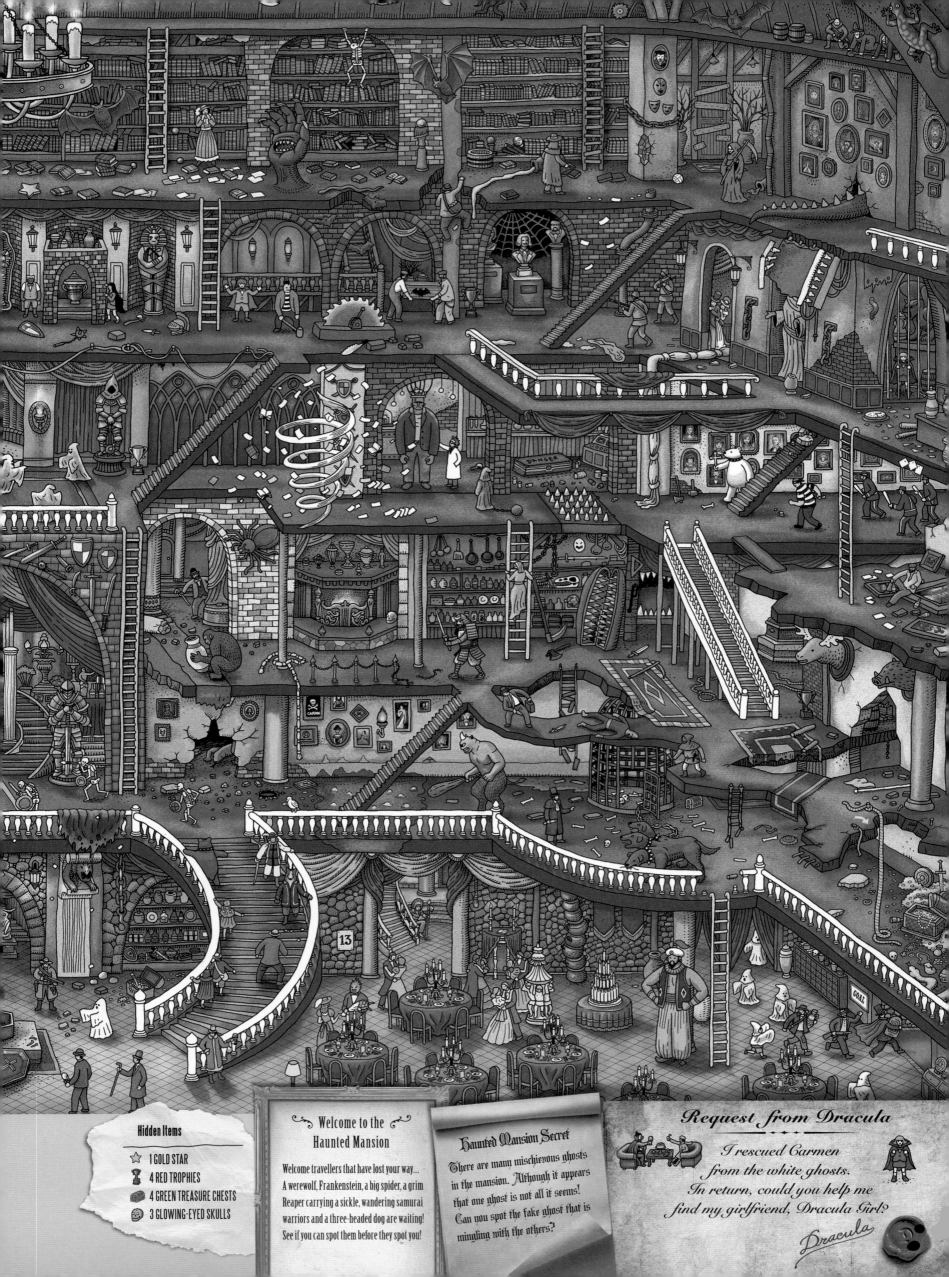

Hidden Items

⭐ 1 GOLD STAR
🏆 4 RED TROPHIES
🟩 4 GREEN TREASURE CHESTS
💀 3 GLOWING-EYED SKULLS

Welcome to the Haunted Mansion

Welcome travellers that have lost your way...
A werewolf, Frankenstein, a big spider, a grim
Reaper carrying a sickle, wandering samurai
warriors and a three-headed dog are waiting!
See if you can spot them before they spot you!

Haunted Mansion Secret

There are many mischievous ghosts
in the mansion. Although it appears
that one ghost is not all it seems!
Can you spot the fake ghost that is
mingling with the others?

Request from Dracula

I rescued Carmen
from the white ghosts.
In return, could you help me
find my girlfriend, Dracula Girl?

Dracula

The Forgotten Town

Thank goodness! Fresh air once more! This is such a pretty town, too.
Make a small detour and ask the dragon statue for Mr X's whereabouts.
Go carefully down the cobbled road: don't trip! Jump from the ledge
of the blue-roofed building onto the neighbouring rooftop. There – look!
It's Mr X's little boat!

Come and join us
Travelling Entertainer's Troupe

Travelling Entertainer's Troupe We are a group of performers travelling the world with our singing and dancing. Wearing purple costumes, we can be found in front of a pink building. Everyone please come and see us!
EMMA, TOMO & SEISHO

SUNDAY MUSICAL

Chocolate House is cause for complaint

The city's residents are all talking about the Chocolate House. However, it is not all good. People are complaining that it is just too well hidden.
Is it actually possible to find it?

To the Sea

Are you ready to set sail? The boat is top-notch; it's a totally dazzling sight! Give a wave to the Pirate Captain who lives on the big island, but sneak quietly behind the octopus, who's in a bad temper today. The goal is behind the raging whirlpool. Hurry, hurry to the jetty…

GOAL

LOADED GUN

MORE HASTE, LESS SPEED

The Witch

SUN KING

GOAL

START

BREAD FAN

$$$$

OUTSIDE

TWINKLE

Agnes

Triumph

RED CAP 6

SHIP GRAVEYARD

CONQUEST

VALOR

TICKET

PIRATES

COME ON

Hidden Items

☆ 2 GOLD STARS

🏆 3 RED TROPHIES

🟩 4 GREEN TREASURE CHESTS

🟥 2 RED TREASURE CHESTS

🐟 1 SWORDFISH

DANGERS: BEWARE!

The ship carrying a green treasure chest is being attacked by pirates! Can the raft with the patched mast really reach the port? A red boat has capsized! Can you see it?

HOW TO BECOME A PIRATE

If you're not prepared,
Don't get on the ship...
To become a pirate,
You must climb the rock fortress
And meet the Pirate Captain!

Advice from the Pirate Captain

A ticket is needed to enter the port. Advance to the next stage after finding nine tickets blowing in the wind. If you don't retrieve them, you will be forced to join my pirate gang.

from the
Pirate Captain

TICKET

A Busy Port

The port is a busy, bustling place. It is full of life – and so noisy! Take care as you cross the jetty, and then be careful not to get caught in the octopus's legs. Mmm…a delicious smell is coming from the seafood restaurant. But there's no time to eat – you must hop on a mine cart to enter the next maze.

Mr X's Port Challenge

Watch out! I have released ten prisoners from their truck. I can't guarantee they won't cause trouble. You can only advance to the next maze when you have found them.

From X

Hidden Items

- ☆ 4 GOLD STARS
- 🏆 4 RED TROPHIES
- 🧰 3 GREEN TREASURE CHESTS
- 🧰 5 RED TREASURE CHESTS
- 🧰 1 BLUE TREASURE CHEST

WELCOME TO THE PORT TOWN

A good place to view the port is from the top of the tower. You can see the boat rental house with a tall chimney and a red roof. The saloon terrace is a good place to rest your legs.

Message from a Citizen

Please help me! I'm looking for my husband! He may be sleeping on the jetty. If you see him, tell him that I'm waiting for him by the saloon. I have a pink parasol.

The Mine Cart Course

Wow! The mountainous mine cart course is just like a rollercoaster! Ready to go? Slowly at first ... but the speed rapidly picks up until you're zooming down the slope. In no time at all the mine cart is swallowed up in the lion's mouth. What will happen now?

CHANGES ON THE COURSE

So many things have changed around here since gold was discovered in these parts. We can now see sunbathers, street performers, a circus tent, a garden party and a hot spring! Can you find them?

Help Farmer Hans

1, 2, 3, 4, 5... oh no, I thought I had 6 cows... I seem to have lost one of them. Where on earth has it gone? Would you please help me find it?

Is dinosaur fossil the elusive Rockosaurus?

A worker has discovered a fossil in the jewel mine. It could be the fossil of the Rockosaurus dinosaur that once lived in the rocky mountain. Can you find the great discovery of the century, too?

Hidden Items

- ☆ 3 GOLD STARS
- 🏆 4 RED TROPHIES
- 🧰 3 GREEN TREASURE CHESTS
- 🧰 1 LUXURIOUS TREASURE CHEST

The Mysterious Market

Well, well! Who'd have thought there'd be a mysterious underground flea market here? Go past a shining statue and weapons that belonged to ancient underground creatures. A staircase near a skirt-eating lizard leads to a pink hotel. Deep in the valley, the entrance to the final maze is in sight.

MESSAGE FROM THE UNDERGROUND SHOPPING UNION

RECENTLY, ILLEGAL TRADING IS ON THE RISE. WATCH OUT FOR THE MAN WITH A RED SUIT AND A RED TOP HAT. IT IS RUMOURED THAT HIS BOX OF WARES IS ACTUALLY EMPTY! CAN YOU FIND HIM?

Museum Director's
SHOPPING LIST

There are so many things that I want from the market: a purple and yellow checked rug, a pink leopard, golden armour and a green Buddha statue. See if you can find them for me.

Request from a Travelling Merchant

While travelling the world, I look for unusual goods for my customers. I'm now looking for a pink tiger. Can you help me?

The Last
Giant Maze

Hooray! At last we can see Mr X's hide-out. But it looks incredibly difficult to reach. Start by turning right, and then right again. Use your detective's intuition. Slipping in front of the yellow clock tower, you'll see another big building. Look – the Maze Stone is there! Grab it, quick!

Hidden Items

- ☆ 5 GOLD STARS
- 🏆 5 RED TROPHIES
- 🧰 5 GREEN TREASURE CHESTS
- 🧍 MR X's SIDEKICK (WEARING BLUE)

Message from Mr X's Sidekick

The Cog Wheel Park is a lovely place for a stroll. I saw a shark in the fishing pond! There are rumoured to be five elephants and a lion around here! I also saw a ghost near the circular tower... Can you find them?

Request from Mr X

At last, you have reached the final maze. However, it would seem that someone has stolen my statue's head. Can you find it and return it?

Golden weathercocks: is the ancient proverb true?

It is said that the person who finds ten golden weathercocks will experience great happiness. Can you find them all?

Maze Stone is safely returned to museum!
Maze Detective saves the day!

Pierre and Carmen are commended by Museum Director, but the Phantom Thief Mr X manages to slip away…

Thanks to Pierre, the Maze Stone was safely retrieved from Mr X Phantom Thief, and was immediately returned to its pedestal in the museum. The world was instantly released from the maze crisis and peace was restored in Opera City. It is reported that the police officers, the countess, the Forest Wizard and the travelling salesman are all delighted.

Further crimes cannot be ruled out, however, as Mr X is still on the loose. When interviewed, Pierre gave a confident smile and did not look concerned. He is, after all, the Maze Detective.

Rockosaurus fossil comes up for auction

A lot of rare items found while the Maze Stone was missing are to be sold at auction. They include the countess's feather hat, Dracula's castle key, the tickets with the Pirate Captain's fingerprints and the very rare Rockosaurus fossil.

There is speculation that the golden weathercock will fetch an all-time record price. Caution may be needed as it is rumoured that expert pickpocket Swift has set his sights on the extremely valuable weathercock.

Message to readers! Is there anything you have missed? Additional maze information now available!

Did you see the travelling entertainers? They were in every scene!

Could you find a dancer in a purple dress, an accordion player and their helpful manager? They were usually performing, but sometimes they were found riding in a balloon or boat…

Rare car, Schmidt T50, is a must-see in Opera City!

It is said that there is only one such car in the world. If you saw it in Opera City you were very lucky indeed.

Will fountains help to revitalize Forgotten Town?

It is hoped that the pretty Forgotten Town can attract more tourists by the addition of nine new fountains scattered in the streets and courtyards.

WANTED!! DEMAND FOR INFORMATION

Mr X's sidekick, the head of the Grammerly family, is on the run! It is rumoured that he is somewhere in the Port Town. If spotted, please inform the police.

QUICK QUIZ

Q1. What animal is the ninja fighting in the Museum?

Q2. As the Town Makes Merry, what animal can be seen on top of the pizza truck?

Q3. In the Open-air Café, what instrument is being played in front of the fountain?

Q4. In Downtown, what colour apron is the flower shop owner wearing?

Q5. At the Balloon Festival, what animal appears on the red and blue balloon?

Q6. In The Castle in the South, which circus animal can be seen?

Q7. In The Haunted Mansion, what item can be found inside the barrel with a key?

Q8. In The Forgotten Town, who is waving to Pierre and Carmen?

Q9. The winner of the yacht race in To the Sea is a green yacht. What number is it?

Q10. What four-digit number is written on the yellow boat in the Port Town?

Q11. What souvenir does the woman in the Port Town buy?

Q12. What message can be read from right-to-left on the building behind Pierre's garage?

Answers 1. **Sabre-toothed tiger** 2. **Pig** 3. **Drums** 4. **Green** 5. **Lion** 6. **Elephant** 7. **Mask** 8. **Dracula** 9. **8** 10. **1920** 11. **Pink Bear** 12. **Get the Golden Star**

'Ahh, now I see!' New light is cast on cases as Maze Detective's routes are revealed!

Reports are in that residents found some of the mazes quite tricky to solve. With Pierre's cooperation, we are able to reproduce the best routes here. The sound of 'Oh, now I understand!' and 'That makes sense!' resounds throughout the town. Requests for even more difficult mazes have been received!

- ■ Maze
- ✕ Mr X's Challenge, Articles, etc.
- ○ Hidden Items
- ○ Other Items
- ○ Additional Maze Information, Quick Quiz Time, etc.

Pierre's Garage

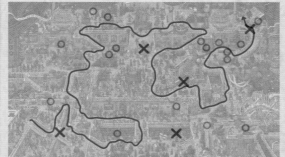
The Museum

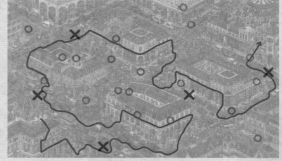
The Town Makes Merry

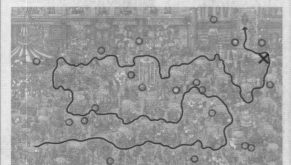
Open-air Café

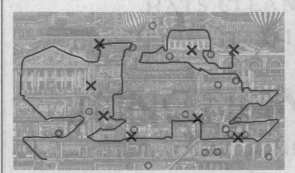
Downtown

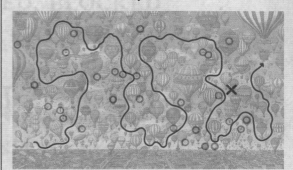
Balloon Festival

The Castle in the South

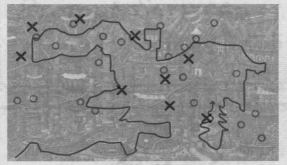
The Mysterious Village in the Forest

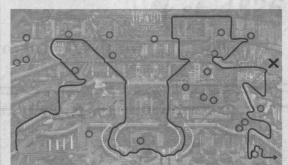
The Haunted Mansion

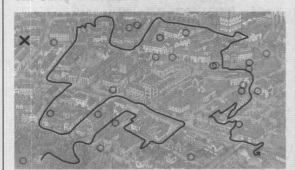
The Forgotten Town

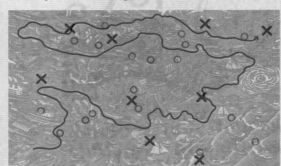
To the Sea

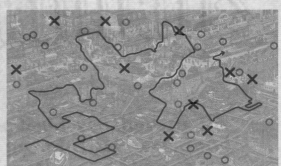
A Busy Port

The Mine Cart Course

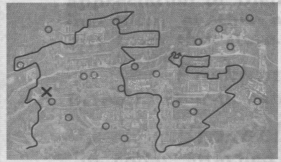
The Mysterious Market

The Last Giant Maze

Pierre The MAZE DETECTIVE

Special Thanks

IC4DESIGN

Daisuke Matsubara
Yoko Sugi
Tatsuya Kawaguchi
Arisa Imamura
Masami Tatsugawa
Keiko Kamigaki

Emma Sakamiya · Naomi Leeman
Benjamin LeMar · Mikiko Matsubara
Andrej Schachtschneider · Agnes Ptak
Anthony-Cédric Vuagniaux
Junichi Nagaoka · Yukihiko Yoshida
Charlotte Cundy Nakamoto · Elizabeth Jenner

Published in 2015 by
Laurence King Publishing Ltd
361–373 City Road
London EC1V 1LR
e-mail: enquiries@laurenceking.com
www.laurenceking.com

© Illustration and text 2015 IC4DESIGN
This book was designed and produced by
Laurence King Publishing Ltd, London.

IC4DESIGN have asserted their right under
the Copyright, Designs and Patents Act of 1988
to be identified as the Author of this Work.

A catalogue record for this book is available
from the British Library.

ISBN: 978-1-78067-563-3

Printed in China